GREAT SCIENTISTS
ISAAC NEWTON

STEVE PARKER

Chrysalis Children's Books

This edition published in 2003 by
Chrysalis Children's Books
64 Brewery Road, London N7 9NT

Copyright © Chrysalis Books PLC
Text © Steve Parker
A Belitha Book

Illustrations/photographs copyright © in this format
by Chrysalis Books PLC

Typeset by Chambers Wallace, London
Printed in Malaysia

British Library Cataloguing in Publication Data
for this book is available from the British Library.

ISBN 1 84138 639 1

Photographic credits:
Bridgeman Art Library 4 Cheltenham Art Gallery
and Museums, Glos., 11 bottom Louvre, Paris,
16 British Museum, London, 17 top Christie's,
London, 19 bottom Museum of the History of
Science, Oxford, 24 top National Trust, Petworth,
Sussex, bottom Guildhall Library, London,
26 Tate Gallery, London
Mary Evans Picture Library 8 top, 9 centre, 14 top
Robert Harding Picture Library 14 bottom
Michael Holford 15 bottom right
Lincolnshire County Council, Isaac Newton
Centre, Grantham Library 5 top, 6
Mansell Collection 8/9 bottom, 9 top, 10
NASA 18 bottom
National Trust Photographic Library 5 bottom,
11 top Tessa Musgrave
Ann Ronan Picture Library/Image Select title page,
20 top and bottom, 23 bottom, 25 top
The Royal Society, London 21 bottom right,
25 bottom
Science Photo Library 13 top Phil Jude, 15
bottom
left, 21 bottom left Ronald Royer, 23 top Michael
Marten, 27 top NASA, bottom Seth Shostak

Illustrations: Tony Smith 6/7, 12, 22
Rodney Shackell 13, 15, 17, 18, 19, 21
Editor: Rachel Cooke
Designer: Andrew Oliver
Picture researcher: Juliet Duff
Specialist adviser: Hillary Ray

Contents

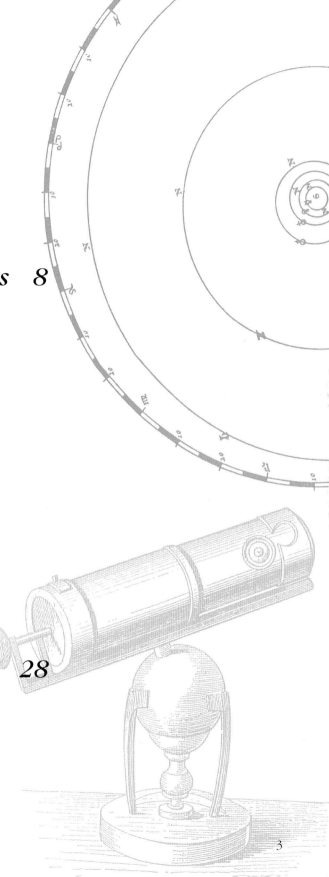

Isaac Newton spent his early years in the rolling countryside of 17th century rural England. The landscape was dotted with farms and villages.

Introduction

Many scientists have been called "great", or even a "genius", but few have been so deserving of these superlatives as Isaac Newton. He made revolutionary advances in many areas of science, from the study of light and colour, to **gravity, forces** and motion, **mechanics, astronomy** and mathematics.

Newton lived at a time when there were many changes happening in science. The traditional teachings of the Ancient Greeks, such as Plato (429-347 BC) and Aristotle (384-322 BC), were no longer accepted without question. People such as Galileo Galilei (1564-1642 AD) had begun a new approach to science: make observations, carry out experiments, test ideas, analyze results, and devise new scientific theories from these various procedures.

Newton drew together many of the theories of this new approach to science. He showed that seemingly different events and processes had the same underlying cause. He introduced a basic framework for the physical sciences that lasted for two hundred years.

Some of Newton's ideas have been overtaken by the work of Albert Einstein (1879-1955) and other modern scientists. But they still have a great effect on the way science explains the workings of the Universe, and the world we live in.

Chapter One
The Early Years

Isaac Newton entered the world in the manor house at Woolsthorpe, near Grantham, Lincolnshire, England. It was Christmas Day, 25 December 1642. The Newton family lived in the manor, although they were not particularly rich. Isaac's father, a farmer also named Isaac, died three months before his son was born. The shock of losing her husband, and the birth of her new baby, made Hannah Newton ill. Isaac himself was premature (born early), small and weak. His mother later told him that he could have been "popped into a quart [two pint] mug".

Despite his frail health, young Isaac survived. When he was three, his mother married again to a wealthy rector, Barnabas Smith. But the next year, when his mother went to live with Rector Smith in a nearby village, Newton stayed behind, to be brought up by his grandmother. It was not until Isaac was ten that his mother returned, widowed once again, with her three children from the second marriage.

Isaac Newton aged twelve.

Woolsthorpe Manor, Newton's birthplace, is now conserved in his honour.

I Newton - carved by the boy himself at school.

Practical Skills

During his childhood, Isaac spent many hours inventing small machines and making models. At grammar school he saved the pocket money sent by his mother to buy saws, hammers and chisels, and wood and other building materials. He made a water clock for his bedroom in the apothecary's attic, and a model of a new windmill in the area. When there was no wind, he put a mouse in the model to make it work. And he experimented with chemicals in the apothecary's cupboards. These were early examples of his practical skills, his inventive nature, and his understanding of mechanical things.

School Days

Isaac learned simple reading, writing and arithmetic at the local school. Being the son of the "lord of the manor", he was expected to go to a grammar school, instead of starting work. This he did, to the Free Grammar School of King Edward VI at Grantham, about 9 km away. During term time he stayed at the home of a Grantham apothecary (chemist or pharmacist).

As a pupil Isaac seemed unexceptional, although there are few historical records of his school days. He was not keen on games, but preferred reading books and making things.

Newton was always competitive. It is said that, at school, when a bully kicked him, he fought back and worked hard to beat the bully in class.

A False Start in Farming

Around the age of 16, Isaac was called back to his mother's home, with the aim of eventually taking over the enlarged family estate. However, he did not make a good farmer. While he was supposed to be tending sheep, he would read books, or carve models from wood, or experiment with water-wheels and dams in the local streams. The sheep wandered into the next field and ate the valuable corn.

After nine months at home, he returned to school in Grantham. He was taught and looked after by the head-master, Henry Stokes. Isaac became head boy, and the teachers prepared him for university. In June 1661 he left home and went to study at Trinity College, part of the University of Cambridge. The town of Cambridge would be his main home for the next 35 years.

Undercurrents of Change

For centuries, scientists and philosophers had accepted the works of Aristotle, Plato and other thinkers from ancient times, which they interpreted in the light of Christian belief and church law. But Newton was being brought up in an atmosphere of change. At the start of the seventeenth century, the English politician and essayist Sir Francis Bacon (1561-1626) had called for a new approach to scientific theory based on factual evidence rather than belief. Weight was given to his ideas by the work of Galileo, who in 1632 showed that the Earth was not the centre of the Universe, as the Bible stated, but that it went around the Sun. This helped to loosen the bonds between science and the Roman Catholic Church. Scientists were no longer prepared to accept old ideas without investigation, and looked for new explanations to the processes they studied.

Chapter Two
University and Its Influences

Changes may have been taking place but, in his early years at Trinity College, Isaac Newton followed a traditional pattern of learning. Students attended lectures in classics (the languages and ways of ancient Greece and Rome), **logic, ethics, rhetoric** and some mathematics.

For his first three years Newton, like many other students, was a "sub-sizar" or poor scholar. He earned his keep by looking after richer students, lecturers and professors. He ran errands, served food, cleaned boots and emptied chamber-pots.

Henry More, the teacher and philosopher, became friendly with Newton at Cambridge. Both came from the Grantham area.

Trinity College, Cambridge is much the same today as in Newton's time. Newton used a shed in the gardens there as a chemistry laboratory.

Reading Revolutionary Works

Encouraged to learn more by the Lucasian Professor of Mathematics at Cambridge, Isaac Barrow, Newton was elected a scholar of Trinity College in 1664. He gained his Bachelor of Arts in January of the next year. By now, his notes show that he was interested in the new ideas in religion, science and **philosophy.** He read books, by the founder of modern philosophy, Frenchman René Descartes (1596-1650), and English thinkers such as Henry More (1614-1687) and Thomas Hobbes (1588-1679).

Newton read widely. He studied the works of German astronomer Johannes Kepler (1571-1630) on light, telescopes and the movement of heavenly bodies. He read Italian scientist Galileo's revolutionary views on mathematics and astronomy. He was strongly influenced by famous English scientist Robert Boyle (1627-1691) and his methods of working, in which experiments and their results formed a vital part of advancing scientific knowledge. He read Boyle's writings on philosophy, chemistry and physics.

Robert Boyle made many advances in science. Boyle's law, relating the volume, pressure and temperature of a gas, is named after him.

Newton also became interested in the various forms of **atomism theory,** suggested by scientists and philosophers such as the Frenchman Pierre Gassendi (1592-1655). These suggested that the Universe is made up of tiny particles of some kind, whose movements and interactions can be studied and predicted mathematically.

Philosopher Pierre Gassendi.

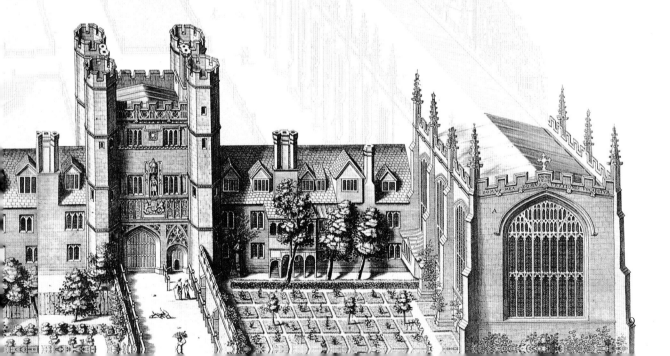

Binomial Series

Some of Newton's early advances in maths involved infinite series. These are sets of numbers or quantities that go on for ever, the simplest being 1, 2, 3, 4, 5 . . . and so on. More complicated is a binomial series, where terms of two numbers or quantities are used. A simple binomial term is $(1 + x)$. The x can be any number you like. Newton devised what he called a rule (mathematical formula) for multiplying a binomial by itself, as many times as you wished, that is, $(1 + x) \times (1 + x) \times (1 + x)$ and so on. You did not have to do all the multiplications, you simply followed the shortcut formula.

Advances in Mathematics

Newton was soon learning mathematics at an amazing speed. He overtook his teachers and went into new areas, studying **geometry** and **algebra.** One of his early advances was a development of the binomial theorem (see panel).

After receiving his Bachelor of Arts qualification, Newton was entitled to four more years at Trinity College, on his own research and study. But college life was brought to an abrupt end in the summer of 1665, when the Plague came to Cambridge.

The terrible and deadly Great Plague of 1665 killed 70,000 people in London alone. The authorities closed important centres of learning, such as Cambridge University, and many students and teachers were sent away. Newton returned to Woolsthorpe in August, to continue his work at the family home.

The Plague ravaged England during 1665-66. Victims were carted away and buried in mass graves in the countryside

Chapter Three
Working Alone

Newton's study at Woolsthorpe, with one of his reflecting telescopes on the table (see page 15).

During two years back in quiet Lincolnshire, Newton worked mainly alone, away from the bustle of university life. Yet this was probably the most important period of his life for scientific thought. Continuing the studies he had made at Cambridge, especially after reading *Principles of Philosophy* by René Descartes, he laid the foundations of his immense breakthroughs in science.

René Descartes

Later in life, he listed the achievement of this period and said: "All this was in the two plague years of 1665-1666. For in those days I was in the prime of my age for invention and minded Mathematiks and Philosophy more than at any time since."

However, he did not publish his work immediately in scientific journals. It came out gradually in various ways, over the following years.

René Descartes

Frenchman René Descartes is known as the founder of modern philosophy. He questioned how we know what exists in reality, as opposed to only in our minds. Central to his work was the approach of doubt or scepticism – only accept something if it seems totally certain and proved beyond all reason. His famous saying was "I think, therefore I am."

Newton used natural light for his experiments: "I . . . made a small hole in my window shuts [blinds], to let in a convenient quantity of the Sun's light . . ."

From White to Colours

Around 1665, Newton became interested in light, and in **optics,** the branch of science dealing with it. He carried out some simple experiments at Woolsthorpe. He shone a narrow beam of sunlight through a **prism.** The light was bent, or **refracted,** as it entered and left the glass. The emerging beam of light that shone onto the wall opposite was wider, and it was split into a **spectrum** - the colours of the rainbow.

At the time, it was accepted that white light was a single pure "substance", an idea of Aristotle's. It could be bent by prisms or bounced off mirrors, but it could not be separated into simpler components. Spectrums through prisms and rainbows through raindrops had been observed but it was thought that the prisms or raindrops added the colour.

The Particle Theory of Light

From his observations, Newton proposed that white light was a mixture of various types of coloured light rays. Each of these was refracted (bent) by a slightly different amount by glass, so they became separated after shining through the prism.

Newton also proposed that light resulted from the movement of tiny particles, or **corpuscles.** Other scientists preferred the idea that light was in the form of pulses or waves. They included Robert Hooke (1635-1703), an English physicist and mathematician, and the Dutch astronomer and natural philosopher Christiaan Huygens (1629-1695), inventor of the pendulum clock. They argued with Newton's conclusions.

However, Newton's corpuscle theory of light backed by his experimental evidence, was taken up by other scientists. It was the main theory of the nature of light until the wave notion became popular again, two hundred years later.

Thousands of raindrops act like tiny prisms to split the Sun's light into its spectrum. The result is the familiar rainbow.

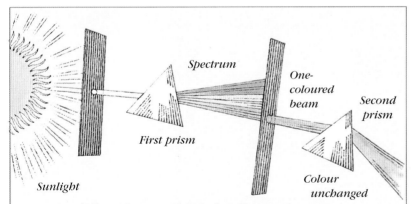

Spectrum

One-coloured beam

Second prism

First prism

Sunlight

Colour unchanged

The Crucial Light Experiment

To confirm his ideas on light, Newton carried out his "crucial experiment". He split light using one prism, blanked off all the resulting colours but one, which he shone through another prism. The emerging beam was wider, but its colour remained pure. He reasoned that all the light rays of one colour were refracted by the same amount, and they could not be split further. At the time, this experiment proved difficult for others to repeat, which fuelled criticism of Newton's work.

Gottfried Leibniz

Who was First?

Through their lives, Newton and his supporters argued with Leibniz and his supporters, about who was first with the techniques of calculus. The disagreements continued for much of the 1700s, between British mathematicians and those in Germany and other parts of mainland Europe.

Leibniz did much of his work independently. But people disagree about whether he "borrowed" some of Newton's ideas. What is certain is that both men contributed greatly to mathematics. Leibniz' term "calculus" lives on, rather than Newton's "fluxions". Also Leibniz' notations or symbols are used today, such as dx and dy for differentiation and $\int$ for integration, rather than Newton's.

Newton returned to the gardens and fountains of Trinity College in 1667, as the Plague receded.

New Links in Mathematics

During the plague years, Newton was also working on different kinds of mathematics. Most famously, he devised a new mathematical technique he called the "method of fluxions" (flowing or changing quantities). Today we call this part of mathematics **calculus** ("calculating"). It involves dealing with numbers that are not constant, but changing.

Some of the mathematical methods in calculus were already known in their simple form. One was **differentiation,** another was **integration.** Newton proposed that differentiation was the "opposite" of integration – an insight which at once made sense of many unconnected bits of mathematics.

This type of work is difficult for non-mathematicians to understand. But it helped to open up a new range of possibilities for scientists. In particular, it could be used to describe the movements of objects, from cannonballs to moons. It was also the cause of a long-running dispute between Newton and the German mathematician Gottfried Leibniz (see panel).

Back to Cambridge

Cambridge University re-opened in the spring of 1667. Newton returned, and was elected a fellow of Trinity College. A still greater honour followed soon after. In 1669, Isaac Barrow retired as Lucasian Professor of Mathematics. Newton, still only 26 years old, was chosen to replace him.

As professor, he was supposed to lecture students on mathematics and science, but Newton never became a great lecturer. Few people came to listen to him. His assistant later said that "so few went to hear him . . . offtimes he did in a manner, for want of hearers, read to the walls".

Newton's New Telescope

After his experiments with light, Newton decided that telescopes using **lenses** would always suffer from a problem, caused by refraction, that made coloured fringes and blurs appear around objects seen through the telescope. Instead, he devised a telescope that used a bowl-shaped mirror. We now call this the Newtonian or reflecting telescope (see panel).

In 1671 he presented an improved version of his telescope to the Royal Society of London. This society, founded only eleven years previously, was already one of the world's most influential scientific centres. He was elected as a Fellow of the Royal Society in 1672.

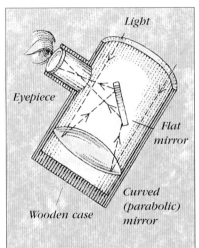

Light

Eyepiece

Flat mirror

Wooden case

Curved (parabolic) mirror

The Newtonian Telescope

Newton's new design for a telescope used a curved mirror to focus the light rays, to form an image. The rays were diverted by another mirror or prism, to the viewer. Newton not only made early versions of the telescope himself, he also made the tools to build it. Many of the world's biggest telescopes today use Newton's basic design.

Newton's own sketch of his telescope design, from about 1670 (far left), and a nine-inch version now housed at London's Science Museum.

A London coffee-house around 1700. Business people, scholars, artists and scientists met at coffee-houses to discuss ideas and exchange information.

Towards Publication

Recognition of his work among scientific circles became increasingly important to Newton. In 1668, he had seen a book by a Danish mathematician, Nicolas Mercator (1620-1687), called *Logarithmotechnia*. It contained mathematical methods that Newton himself had devised a few years earlier. Although Mercator had worked them out separately, Newton wanted people to realize that he had developed the ideas first.

At the time, one way of being noticed was to write a letter to another mathematician. The ideas it contained would then be circulated through scientific societies, meetings and, less formally, coffee-houses. So Newton set down his ideas in a letter, known as *De analysi,* and sent it to mathematician John Collins (1625-1683).

Newton followed this with other letters and articles. However, his competitive nature led to lengthy battles with fellow scientists. Foremost among his opponents was Robert Hooke. Already a well-known scientist, Hooke made some critical remarks on an article on optics Newton published in 1672.

Newton reacted badly to criticism. For a while, he worked almost in isolation. But, in 1675, believing Hooke to have accepted his ideas, Newton wrote *An Hypothesis Explaining the Properties of Light.* This time Hooke accused Newton of stealing his ideas. Despite the efforts of other scientists, the two were now enemies.

Chapter Four
Gravity and Motion

In the 1670s, Newton worked less on optics and mathematics. instead he studied chemistry and **alchemy.** He also spent much time reading about religions and **theology** – the study of the existence of God, his nature and his purpose. He examined the timespan of creation according to the Bible, ancient Hebrew writings, and many theological books.

Still bubbling, too, were the many thoughts and ideas Newton had considered during the plague years of 1665-66. At that time, he looked at why things move as they do and devised the three laws of motion in their basic form. It is difficult to imagine science today without them. Later, they were published in Newton's book, the *Principia* (see Chapter Five).

An alchemist at work.

The Three Laws of Motion

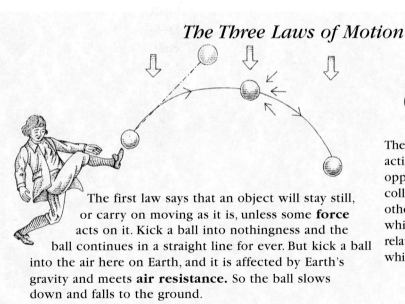

The first law says that an object will stay still, or carry on moving as it is, unless some **force** acts on it. Kick a ball into nothingness and the ball continues in a straight line for ever. But kick a ball into the air here on Earth, and it is affected by Earth's gravity and meets **air resistance.** So the ball slows down and falls to the ground.

The third law says that for every action there is an equal and opposite reaction. If two balls collide and rebound off each other, the combined speeds at which they rebound will be related to the combined speeds at which they collided.

The second law of motion says that if a force acts on an object, the object moves in the direction of that force. And the object's acceleration is related to the "strength" of the force, and to the **mass** of the object. Kick a ball, and it moves off in the direction you kick it. Kick it harder, and it accelerates faster. Kick a big, heavy ball, and it goes slower than a small, light ball.

The Falling Apple

It is said that the idea of gravity as a universal force came to Newton during the plague years, as he sat in the family garden at Woolsthorpe. He watched an apple fall – some versions say it fell onto his head – and wondered why it was attracted to the Earth. Although there are many accounts of this story, and Newton mentions apples in his writings, it is not possible to say whether it is true or false.

Earth seen from the Moon. "I began to think of gravity extending to the orb of the Moon," wrote Newton.

Ideas about Gravity

Newton used his ideas to explain the motions of moons and planets. At that time, these were explained in various ways. The basis of Descartes' view was that they were caught in vortices, or "whirlpools", of tiny particles. Newton was beginning to think instead about some form of invisible attraction between these objects. The bigger an object, in terms of its mass (the matter it contained), the greater its force in attracting other objects. The Earth, being enormous, would have a very strong force that pulled things towards its centre. We now call this force gravity.

Newton imagined that the Earth's gravitational force spread far into space, all the way to the Moon. He proposed that the curved path of one object around another, such as the Moon around the Earth, resulted from two balanced forces. One was the **centripetal force,** pulling the object towards the centre of the circle. The other was the **centrifugal force,** pulling it away from the centre. To prove his theories, Newton then analyzed circular motion mathematically.

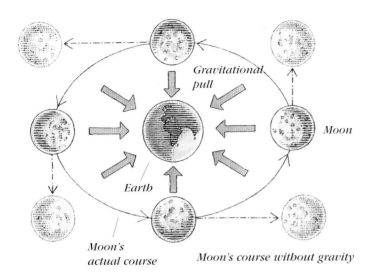

Gravitational pull

Moon

Earth

Moon's actual course

Moon's course without gravity

The centripetal force of Earth's gravity keeps the Moon orbiting the Earth. "Switch off" gravity and the Moon would continue in a straight line, flying off into space.

Centripetal Force

Newton's proposal about centrifugal force enabled him to go on to great work. But today, most scientists believe that centrifugal force does not exist. Imagine twirling a ball on a string, round and round. According to Newton's first law of motion, the ball should go in a straight line, unless some force acts on it. There is a force – the pull of the string, which continuously drags the ball around in a circle. This is the centripetal force. There is no need for a centrifugal force pulling the ball outwards, since the ball's tendency to go straight provides this.

Suddenly, the string breaks! The centripetal force disappears. Freed from it, the ball goes off in a straight line, according to Newton's first law. But the Earth's own gravity and **friction** from the air cause the ball gradually to slow down and fall to the ground, according to Newton's second law.

The Moon's **orbit** around the Earth can be explained in the same way. According to Newton's first law of motion, the Moon would go in a straight line through the nothingness of space, unless some force acted on it. That force is the Earth's gravity, which continuously pulls the Moon towards the Earth. This gravity balances the Moon's own tendency to go in a straight line, away into space. And so the Moon endlessly orbits the Earth.

During Newton's time, star-gazing and comet-spotting became fashionable pastimes.

Chapter Five

The Principia

PHILOSOPHIÆ
NATURALIS
PRINCIPIA
MATHEMATICA

Autore JS. NEWTON, Trin. Coll. Cantab. Soc. Matheseos Professore Lucasiano, & Societatis Regalis Sodali.

IMPRIMATUR·
S. PEPYS, Reg. Soc. PRÆSES.
Julii 5. 1686.

LONDINI,
Jussu Societatis Regiæ ac Typis Josephi Streater. Prostat apud plures Bibliopolas. Anno MDCLXXXVII.

The title page of the first part of the Principia

"There is one thing more that I thought to inform you of . . . that Mr Hooke has some pretensions upon the invention of the rule of the decrease of gravity being reciprocally as the squares of the distances from the centre. He says you had the notion from him . . ."

So wrote the young astronomer Edmund Halley (1656-1742) to Newton in May, 1686. His letter reported that the Royal Society had agreed to publish the book that Newton was then writing. This was called *Philosophiae naturalis principia mathematica* ("The Mathematical Principles of Natural Philosophy"), usually simply known as the *Principia*.

In his letter, Halley said that Robert Hooke was claiming some credit for the **inverse square law.** This is one of the most important laws of science (see panel on page 22).

Newton chairs a meeting at the Royal Society in about 1710. It was the Royal Society that published the Principia.

More Rivalry

It was partly the rivalry between himself and Hooke that had spurred Newton into writing the *Principia* in the first place. In 1679, Hooke suggested the ideas of a deflecting centripetal force and the inverse square law, when dealing with planets. But he could not provide the mathematics to support his proposals. And he thought gravity was a specific force that happened only in certain cases, not a universal feature of all matter, all of the time.

When asked by Halley about Hooke's claims, Newton said that he had already done the sums years before, but he could not find them. He wrote them out again and presented them as a scientific article called *De motum corporum in gyrum* ("On the Motion of Revolving Bodies").

In his calculations, Newton used the **laws of planetary motion** worked out by Kepler about sixty years previously. He showed that the inverse square law explained many features of planetary motion, such as how the planets moved in ellipses ("ovals") rather than in true circles. Halley (clerk to the Royal Society) and other supporters encouraged Newton to write a full-length book. It took him about two years, and the result was the *Principia,* published in 1687.

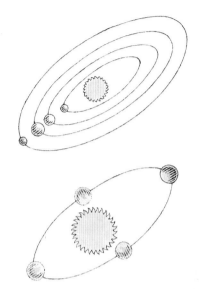

The Earth does not go in circles around the Sun. Its orbit is elliptical ("oval"). This is also true of other planets in the Solar System.

Edmund Halley

One of Newton's chief supporters, Edmund Halley (right) catalogued the positions of stars, analyzed their movements, and proposed that comets make very long but very regular trips around the Sun, so that their re-appearance can be predicted accurately. In 1704 he became Professor of Geometry at Oxford, and in 1720 he took over from John Flamsteed as Astronomer Royal.

The comet (left) which Halley spotted in 1682, and which returns every 76 years, is named after him.

Newton's Law of Gravitation

Newton's universal law of gravitation states:

• Any object or piece of matter, from a planet to a pinhead, has an attracting or gravitational force.

• The gravitational force between two objects is proportional to the product of their masses – that is, their masses ("weights") multiplied together.

• The gravitational force varies with the distance between the two objects. Very simply, the gravitational force of an object fades extremely quickly as you get farther from it. Mathematically, the force fades according to the inverse square of the distance. (In maths, a square is a number multiplied by itself, while the inverse square is that number divided into one.) if the distance between two objects is doubled, the force between them is reduced to one-fourth. If the distance is tripled, the force is reduced to one-ninth, and so on.

The formula is

$$F = G m_1 m_2 / r^2,$$

where F is the gravitational force, G is the gravitational constant (a special number which is always the same), m1 and m_2 are the masses of the two objects and r is the distance between them.

Newton had many discussions with Halley concerning his theories about gravity and the movement of the planets.

The Success of the Principia

Many times, the *Principia* has been called "the greatest scientific book ever written". Even as he was working on it, Newton realized that the laws of motion and universal gravitation could explain many varied processes and events, from the orbits of planets around the Sun, to swinging pendulums, bullets fired from a gun, objects bouncing off each other, the rise and fall of the sea's tides, and things falling to the Earth's surface. It was about this time that the term "gravitas" (heaviness or weight) came into more common use.

Newton wrote the *Principia* in Latin, which was the language of proper scientific communication. The first of the three parts sets out his three laws of motion (see page 17) and describes the orbits of planets. The second discusses how fluids flow, and why Descartes' "whirlpools" could not explain the movements of moons and planets. The third deals with the idea that gravity depends on mass. It shows how the theory of gravitation can be applied to planets orbiting the Sun, the "wobbles" of the Moon's orbit, the strange-shaped paths of comets, and many other astronomical oddities.

What is Gravity?

With the publication of the *Principia*, science had a simple set of laws and rules to describe many apparently unconnected events. The world has rarely seen such moments. But exactly what caused gravitational attraction? Newton said that his work described what happened, not how. For the cause, he suggested a new version of an old idea. An unseen and undetectable substance, the **ether,** was involved. These ideas of a new ether were followed by many scientists over the years but gradually faded. The true nature of gravity is still being debated today.

The Moon's gravitational attraction pulls a "bulge" of water toward it. As the Moon orbits the Earth, it pulls the bulge around, too. We see this in the rise and fall of the tides.

The Principia *was a huge success. This drawing, showing the study of Newton's rings (see page 25), is from a simplified version published in 1747.*

Chapter Six
Newton's Later Years

After the immense efforts and effects of the *Principia*, Newton's scientific career was almost over. In 1693, he suffered a mental breakdown. He would often go for days without sleeping because of taxing astronomical observations at night. In addition, one of his closest friendships, with the young Swiss mathematician Fatio de Duillier, had ended a few months before.

Perhaps a breakdown of this kind was inevitable. Through his life, Newton was often awkward in social situations. He was a strong **Protestant,** he never married, and he avoided women. He wrote to his friend, the philosopher John Locke: "Being of the opinion that you endeavoured to embroil me with woemen … when one told me you were sickly and would not live, I answered twere better if you were dead."

He could be charming and friendly at some times, but aggressive and abusive at others. He was very sensitive to criticism. This spilled over from normal scientific debates into long, bitter, personal attacks on his rivals, such as Hooke and Leibniz.

During the 1680s-90s, Newton left science. He became a well-known figure in public life.

The Royal Mint and the Tower of London. Newton was a very thorough Master of the Mint, catching many money-forgers.

Warden of the Mint

Newton slowly recovered. He pursued his interest in religious and political matters. From 1689-90, he had been Member of Parliament for Cambridge University. Now, in 1696, he was appointed Warden of the Royal Mint, and three years later he became Master of the Mint. His job was to oversee a whole new range of coins being introduced in England. Newton followed forgers and counterfeiters with amazing energy, sending some to their deaths. Around 1700 he moved from Cambridge to London.

In 1703, Newton was elected President of the Royal Society. In 1704, only after the death of Robert Hooke, did he accept the post and publish his book *Opticks.* This explained his further ideas on light and colours, and contained a description of the rainbow-like patterns seen in pieces of glass pressed close together. These interference patterns are called **Newton's rings,** and are familiar today in thin layers of oil spilled on the road.

The First Scientist Knight

Newton became science's first "Sir" when he was knighted in 1705 by Queen Anne. A second edition of the *Principia* was published in 1713, and a third in 1726. The next year on 31 March, Newton died in London. He was buried with huge ceremony in Westminster Abbey. Newton's achievements in so many areas are reflected by the design of his tomb, erected in 1731 in the Abbey. its carved stonework includes a telescope, furnace, prism, coins, the Earth and planets and Sun, mathematical numbers, and books labelled *Chronology, Optica, Divinity* and *Phil. Princ. Math.*

John Flamsteed (1646-1719)

The first Astronomer Royal at the Greenwich Observatory (above), from 1675 to 1719, Flamsteed made lists and charts of the stars and their movements, mainly to help navigation at sea. The charts were many times more accurate than the previous versions. The data he provided helped Newton with his work but the two soon fell out. This was partly because Flamsteed wanted to keep his star information until it was completed, but Newton and Halley tried to publish some of it – and without giving Flamsteed credit.

Chapter Seven
Newton in Perspective

Isaac Newton has been called "the culminating figure in the Scientific Revolution of the seventeenth century". At the time, his work seemed to open up a whole new era of scientific thought. As the poet Alexander Pope (1688-1744) wrote: "Nature and Nature's Laws lay hid in Night: God said Let Newton Be! and All was Light." However, as a result of the long arguments between Newton and his supporters, and Leibniz and his supporters, there was a rift between some scientists in Britain and those in mainland Europe. This gradually healed, and over the following years the "New Newtonians" took his work to Europe, and into the centre of mainstream science.

The Language of Science

Like the famous Galileo, Newton realized that the basic language of science was mathematics. So he used mathematics to describe his main laws and discoveries. And he acknowledged his debt to Galileo and others, saying: "If I have seen further, it is by standing on the shoulders of giants."

In William Blake's painting Newton, *the dividers are a symbol of geometry and mathematics. Isaac Newton's achievements were a popular subject for artists and poets in the 18th century.*

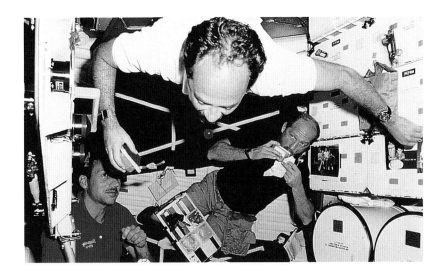

Earth's gravity is so familiar that we take it for granted. When astronauts go into space, the combination of the spacecraft's motion and the much weaker gravity makes them feel "weightless".

An artist's impression of a communications satellite in space. The height and speed that such satellites need to keep them in orbit is calculated by Newtonian mathematics.

In a simple way, Newton viewed the Universe as a gigantic clockwork machine that worked according to a few straightforward principles. For well over a century, his laws and mathematical equations were used by scientists everywhere. His predictions that comets went around the Sun in immense oval-shaped orbits, and that the Earth was not a true sphere but slightly flattened at the poles, were shown to be true.

From Newton to Einstein

Gradually, observations were collected that did not quite fit the Newtonian view. Scientists peering inward to the basic pieces of matter – **atoms,** and the even tinier bits inside them – found that Newton's laws did not seem to work on such a small scale. The orbit of the planet Mercury, near the Sun, did not exactly fit Newton's laws either. Astronomers suggested Mercury was being disturbed by the gravity of a planet even closer to the Sun, which they wanted to call Vulcan. They looked for it, but without success. Similarly, experiments on the speed and nature of light did not fit precisely with Newtonian physics.

Finally, the work of many scientists was brought together by Albert Einstein (1879-1955), with his theories of special relativity in 1905, and general relativity in 1916. But the less complex "clockwork mechanics" of Isaac Newton are still sufficient to explain gravity, motion and most of what happens in the world around us.

The World in Newton's Time

	1625-1650	1651-1657

Science

1625-1650	1651-1657
1628 William Harvey publishes his description of how the heart pumps blood around the body	1655 John Wallis publishes *Arithmetica infinitorum* one of the stages in the development of calculus
1637 René Descartes publishes *Discours de la Méthode*	1656 Christiaan Huygens designs one of his first improved pendulum clocks
1642 Galileo Galilei dies	1660 The Royal Society is founded in London
1642 Isaac Newton is born	

Exploration

1625-1650	1651-1657
1626 New Amsterdam, eventually New York, is founded on the banks of the Hudson River	1659 Christiaan Huygens studies Mars with an improved telescope
1643 Abel Tasman reaches Tonga ("Friendly Isles") and Fiji in the Pacific	1662 The Kongo kingdom in West Africa is destroyed by the Portuguese
	1673 Jacques Marquette reaches the headwaters of the Mississippi River

Politics

1625-1650	1651-1657
1625 Charles I becomes King of England and marries Henrietta Maria of France	1651 Last battle in English Civil War. Charles II flees to France
1642 The Civil War begins in England; Charles I against supporters of Oliver Cromwell	1660 Charles II returns to the English throne as the monarchy is restored
1648 Thirty Year War of religion ends in Europe	1666 Great Fire of London

Art

1625-1650	1651-1657
1631 Architect Inigo Jones begins work on London's Covent Garden square and market (completed 1635)	1661 French play writer Molière finishes *L'école des femmes*
1642 Rembrandt finishes his largest work, *Night Watch*	1667 John Milton writes his famous poem *Paradise Lost*
1648 Building of the Taj Mahal in India completed	1672 Chinese ink picture *Autumn Landscape* painted by Kao Ts'en

1676 Robert Hooke discovers a rule relating the stretch of a spring to the tension in it, now known as Hooke's law

1679 Gottfried Leibniz introduces the idea of binary numbers

1698 Thomas Savery makes an early steam engine, to pump water from mines

1679 Louis Hennepin is the first European to see Niagara Falls

1682 Edmund Halley sees the comet named after him

1690s Gold and gems are discovered in Brazil, beginning a gold rush

1683 The Turks lay siege to Vienna

1689 William of Holland and Mary become King and Queen of England, in the Glorious Revolution

1690 Battle of the Boyne in Ireland

1678 John Bunyan's *The Pilgrim's Progress* is published

1689 Henry Purcell produces the first English opera, *Dido and Aeneas*

1701 Jethro Tull invents a machine, the seed drill, for planting seeds

1714 Daniel Gabriel Fahrenheit invents a scale for temperature

1727 Isaac Newton dies

1703 Peter the Great, Tsar of Russia, founds the city of Saint Petersburg

1722 Easter Island in the Pacific, one of the world's most remote islands, is discovered by Jakob Roggeveen

1707 England and Scotland join together

1713 War of Spanish Succession ends with Treaty of Utrecht

1715 Louis XIV (King of France) dies after the longest reign of any European monarch (since 1643)

1709 The first pianos are made in Florence by Bartolomeo Cristofori

1719 Daniel Defoe writes *Robinson Crusoe*

1721 Johann Sebastian Bach composes his *Brandenburg Concertos*

Glossary

air resistance: the *force* that slows an object moving through air, due to the object colliding with atoms and molecules of the gases in air.

alchemy: the ancient science which studied substances and how they were made up. It is associated with magic, but, practised seriously, it was in effect an early form of chemistry.

algebra: the branch of mathematics in which quantities can be unknown, and are represented by general symbols, like the letters x and y. In the algebraic sum $2 + x = 5$, then x must be 3.

astronomy: the study of the planets, moons, stars and other objects in space.

atomism theory: the proposal that everything in the Universe is made up of tiny particles (*called atoms or corpuscles*) of some kind. The theory has had many forms through the ages, and scientists today believe one version of it.

atoms: the smallest part of a substance, far too tiny to see under the most powerful microscope. Atoms can be split into smaller particles, such as electrons and neutrons, but these no longer have the physical and chemical features of the original substance.

calculus: a branch of mathematics which uses calculations and equations to find lengths, areas and volumes, and how these change with time.

centrifugal force: a force that pulls an object moving in a circle away from the centre. It is now regarded as a non-existent or "fictional" force. See *centripetal force*.

centripetal force: a force that pulls an object moving in a circle toward the centre. The Earth's *gravity* provides the centripetal force that tries to pull the Moon toward it, balancing the Moon's tendency to go in a straight line.

corpuscles: a general name for tiny particles, bodies or objects. Atoms have been called corpuscles in the past, as are the microscopic cells in blood today.

differentiation: a procedure in calculus that deals with and describes numbers or amounts that are always changing. For example, differentiation allows one to calculate the varying speed of a racing car as it continually slows down and speeds up around the track.

ether: in the past, this was thought to be an unseen, undetectable substance which was present everywhere. Its existence has been proposed for various reasons, such as carrying light rays or magnetism. However, modern science no longer accepts the idea of an ether.

ethics: the area of human thought and behaviour concerned with right and wrong, good and bad, and similar moral questions. It also covers the rules and principles we invent concerning these topics.

force: something that can make an object change its direction, its rate of movement or its shape. A force is obviously applied when a foot kicks a ball or a rope pulls a car. Some forces are less easy to spot, such as *gravity* and magnetism. The modern unit of force is the newton.

friction: the force that slows down movement when one surfaces passes over another. Rougher surfaces produce greater friction. A ball kicked along the ground will eventually stop, partly because of **air resistance** but mostly because of friction between the ball and the ground.

geometry: a branch of mathematics which deals with lines, flat shapes, such as circles and squares, and solid shapes, such as spheres and cubes. It uses mathematical equations to find lengths, areas, volumes and other features.

gravity (gravitational attraction): the attraction or pulling force between one object and another. It is one of the fundamental forces of nature, and all objects possess it. But it is usually used to describe the vast gravitational attraction exerted by the Earth, that pulls smaller objects towards its centre. Earth's gravity pulls you to the ground when you jump into the air.

integration: a procedure in calculus that deals with, adds up and otherwise manipulates very tiny numbers, quantities or amounts.

inverse square law: a mathematical formula with several uses in science, such as working out the intensity of light, the strength of an electric charge, and the strength of gravitational attraction. In the last, as the two objects get farther apart, the force of attraction decreases according to 1 divided by the square of the distance between them. (An inverse is one divided by a number, and a square is a number multiplied by itself.) So force = 1/(distance x distance).

laws of planetary motion: mathematical explanations, worked out by Johannes Kepler around 1609-19, which show how and why the planets move in ellipses ("ovals") rather than in true circles, and how fast they travel.

lenses: pieces of transparent material such as glass or plastic, specially shaped to alter the direction of light rays.

logic: using reasoned thought, analysis and deduction to come to decisions and viewpoints, without having to rely on beliefs or ideas that cannot be proven.

mass: in everyday terms, the amount of matter in an object. The scientific definition involves the object's resistance to acceleration. Mass is different from weight, which depends on the gravitational force acting on the object. An astronaut has the same mass on the Moon and on the Earth, but his weight differs.

mechanics: the study of how matter and objects behave when acted on by forces. The objects can be tiny, such as atoms, or fluids, such as water, or familiar things like snooker balls.

Newton's rings: rainbow-like patterns seen in pieces of glass or similar substances pressed close together, where there is a diminishing gap between them. They are due to interference patterns in light waves.

optics: the study of light.

orbit: the path traced out by one object going around another, such as a moon going around a planet, or a planet going around a star.

philosophy: the study of human knowledge, beliefs and thoughts. it affects many aspects of our lives, such as how we know things, why we believe in right and wrong, and why we think some things valuable but others worthless.

prism: a piece of glass with flat surfaces at angles to each other, usually a triangular wedge shape.

Protestant: a non-Catholic member of the Western Christian Church, who follows the principles set down during the Reformation of the 16th Century. During this time and later, new branches of the Church developed that did not accept the Pope as their religious leader or the Roman Catholic laws he represented.

refracted: when light is bent as it travels at an angle from one substance to another, as from air into water or glass.

rhetoric: the study of how to use speech, written words and other forms of language effectively, often to persuade others.

spectrum: the "colours of the rainbow" from red to violet that make up white light.

theology: the study of religions and their gods, their nature and how people think of them.

Index